WELCOME LIGHT

D1507729

WELCOME LIGHT

POEMS BY

Paul Kane

AUDUBON TERRACE PRESS
New York

ISBN 978-0-9972547-0-9
Library of Congress Control Number: 2016932038

Cover painting by Neville Pilven
Design by Rita Lascaro

Published in New York, NY by Audubon Terrace Press
Manufactured in the United States of America

First Edition

Contents

Acknowledgements

Several poems in this book originally appeared in journals, anthologies, and other publications, as follows.

"Hard Light in the Goldfields" and "Hafiz Ghazal 179," *Alhambra Poetry Calendar;* "Co. Kerry," *Australian Book Review* and *Best Australian Poems 2013;* "The Wind at Your Back," *Axon;* "Triangulating the Tasman," *Best Australian Poems 2011;* "From *Eugene Onegin* V:1," *Cartographic Electric;* "A Trace of Doubt," *The Common;* "Hafiz Ghazal 75," *Cordite;* "Hafiz Ghazal 373," *Love Among the Ruins;* "On a Mountaintop at Night," *Harvard Review;* "A Light Breeze is Best," *Digital Bridge: New Zealand Electronic Poetry Centre* and *The turnrow Anthology of Contemporary Australian Poetry,* edited by John Kinsella (Monroe, LA: turnrow Books, 2014); "At a Crossroads near Delphi," *PAN: Philosophy Activism Nature;* "K and the Birds," *Sufi;* "The Genoa Grail," *Quadrant.* The following appeared in *A Slant of Light* (Geelong: Whitmore Press, 2008): "Nothing Gold Can Stay," "An Invitation," "The Grand Tour 1968," "Past Coober Pedy," "A Constant Refrain," and "Travels with F. E." "Seven Catastrophes in Four Movements" and "Co. Kerry" appear on the CD *Seven Catastrophes in Four Movements,* with music by Katie O'Looney (Dublin: Farpoint Recordings, 2013). Versions of Hafiz appeared in *Hafiz: Twelve Ghazals* (Warwick, NY: Warwick Publications, Inc., 2014), with illustrations by Tina Kane. The following appeared in *The Scholar's Rock: Selected Poems in Chinese Translation* (Nanjing, China: Otherland Publishing, 2011): "Triangulating the Tasman," "An Invitation," "K Goes to the Supermarket," "The Imagined World," and "Recognition." "VFGA" was shortlisted for the Peter Porter Poetry Prize and published in *Australian Book Review.*

Grateful acknowledgement is made to the Susan Turner Fund at Vassar College for assistance with this book; to the Guesthouse Arts Cooperative in Cork, Ireland, for an artist-in-residence grant; and to the Bogliasco Foundation for its generous support during a residency at the Liguria Study Center for the Arts and Humanities. Special thanks to Bhisham Bherwani for his assistance in bringing the project to fruition.

To Tina

I am Thou,
Thou art I

"WORDS IS ENIGMAS"

—Emily, Lady Tennyson
Journal entry, 1 Feb. 1867

I write this poem over and over—
it never stays written. At night,
with the house closed up, some revenant
steals the meaning from the words.
Next morning, with an empty heart,
I start the process again.
"Words is enigmas," said the wife in despair.
How else to make sense of what connects us
to the world? From the window seat
overlooking the stream, the coverlet
is the blue of the sky and the water. The red
cushion the color of barn siding, even
the green binding of the book beside me speaks
to the cedar tree and a few straggling leaves.
It is the sun that embraces it all, drawing out
the hue with improbable white light.
All this I put into the poem, but
when darkness comes and the stars put
the moon to bed, the intercessor arrives,
throwing, across the frame of today, the shuttle
back and forth in reverse, that the world
begin again, with sunrise and the transit
of our star across the sky. All this
does make sense, somehow, in the moment
it's written down, when the enigma takes over
and the poem seems once again complete
for the half-life of its day.

I

The Poet K

K AND THE BIRDS IN WINTER

The poet K has fed more birds
    than Saint Francis of Assisi.

Each day scattering sunflower seeds
    he fills feeders for his flock.

The birds know K and sing his verses
    to one another as their own.

Chickadees honor K in mobbing
    the evergreens; robins puff up

and hunker down in the woods
    until K announces his poems of spring.

In the field beyond the stream, below
    his nook of glass, K notes how scores

of redwing blackbirds shred the matted
    grass in snow melt. Titmouse and finch

bob on bare branches, keeping time for K,
    as he taps out rhythms for his poems.

WHAT WE HEAR OF THE POET K

The poet K is known to have a way with words:
his cats purr at certain syllables, such as foo and wa,
and even at the purer vowels: a, e, i, o, u and
sometimes y. A single word can stop a dog in its
wayward tracks or make it sit, shake hands, lie down,
roll over. But his images affect people most:
he can dumbfound a loquacious waiter, defrost
a bureaucrat, dissuade a telemarketer.
At a line from a poem, Adventists at his doorstep
kneel to be shriven; children weep.
The poet K no longer trusts the mails: postal workers
cannot bear to hand over his letters, precious beyond words.
And yet no one in the town has ever seen the poet K,
or so they think: they do not recognize him, he is so
ordinary. But his words, afloat upon the air,
are like sounds not quite heard or reminiscent smells
subliminal, sights hardly glimpsed. As the poet K
walks the streets, people he passes—one by one—detach
from cell phones and ear buds, look up for a moment,
as if the world were suddenly no longer theirs alone.

K GOES TO THE SUPERMARKET

Wherever the poet K goes, there is a buzz.
As he walks the aisles with a shopping cart
bags of pasta straighten themselves,
cans of Campbell's soup turn their labels out,
the produce murmurs admiringly,
meat sighs behind glass.

To be the chosen one—that is the desire
of the entire store. An apple nearly bursts
with pride, picked up. A cantaloupe weeps,
finding itself too hard. Corn can barely
restrain itself, waving golden tassels.

K is not indifferent to these displays, merely
intent upon his chore. He knows the power
poetry holds over vegetable and animal kingdoms.
K glides mute with his cart through the store,
careful not to incite riot or induce rot.

THE POET K VISITS THE UROLOGIST

"And that's where the sperm comes out," she says,
pointing at the monitor (a square Sony box on a trolley).
The prostate had suddenly come into view in the canal trip
through his nether parts. His cicerone, the doctor, seemed pleased.
And why not? It was going well. K himself was inclined
to inner journeys, so this one was nothing unique.
Together they had wended through the channel of the penis,
spelunking through the roseate sphincter ("take a deep breath"),
and now, past the headlands of the prostate, were at last emerging
into the wide chamber of the bladder, with its fleshy, veined walls,
its water bubbles coalescing, and—buried deep in the crevices—
the caverns that led to the kidneys, from whence there now issued
tiny translucent spheres of urine. "O, what a good drinker you are,"
exclaims the enigmatic nurse, while the doctor coos like a tourist, flipping
her little camera around. K smiles upon his companions, for this
is territory he already knows inside and out, having imagined it
once in a poem, as if giving birth to himself. Nothing, with K,
goes to waste. Relaxed, reclined upon the table as in a deck chair,
K is beyond pain or discomfort (only the inserted Novocain jelly
had burned at first). He knew—had known all along—that this
was more about the doctor, some routine she was given to, her
cool deft handling suggestive of professions other than her own.

THE POET K VISITS LIGURIA

As the Poet K watched the swirling seawater—
white and foaming as it broke against the rocks—

he thought of the lacework on old gowns,
how delicate it was and intricate, as if

the maker had all the time in the world.
K felt that he, too, had time on his hands,

imagined it spooling onto small wooden bobbins,
its fine silk and linen threads his to manipulate,

to braid into a deceptively simple design,
its recurring pattern imperceptible to most

though apparent to the patient eye.
K looked on as, far below, one wave after

another, in turning to white water on the dark rocks,
exalted them before resolving into foam,

and he thought again about those subtle threads
and how one day they would need to be cut.

K THE REVIVALIST

Every fortnight, under a pseudonym, the poet K
sermonizes the local evangelical church.
Revered—though not a reverend—and feared,
he thinks the parishioners doth protest too much.
Calm in his delivery—like Jonathan Edwards
gazing fixedly upon a hempen rope hanging
from the belfry—the poet K stirs up
the sludge at the bottom of the soul:
young and old shake and begin to swoon,
longing to grasp his words, till driven
into the aisles on hands and knees
in an ecstasy of pain, they reach out, begging
him please to stop. The poet K
smiles inwardly at how much the clamor
resembles his very best poetry readings.

II

Triangulations

THE GRAND TOUR 1968

The first Aussie I ever met
quit the youth hostel in Tunis
the night we boarded the ferry
bound for Naples on New Year's Eve.
She was blonde, pretty and tan
and laughed a lot after bottles
of champers on the tipsy boat.
Hooked up with a fellow from
upstate New York—who feigned
annoyance at her fawning and favors—
the three of us headed straight for Rome
and thence to the Alps in a car
that got stuck in a snow bank at moonrise.
The funniest thing she'd ever seen—
having never seen snow before—
we pushed the car and slipped
and fell, and all she could do
was lie there and laugh and laugh
as if life were a joyful absurdity.

TRIANGULATING THE TASMAN

(i) Warwick

A point has no dimension: the bird in flight across the field
describes a line, but does not exist anywhere on that line.

The cardinal is a red point, the jay a blue.
Here, everything is contained in its momentary immensity.

When we leave for the airport, in anticipation,
uncertain with regret, we enter time.

(ii) Talbot, Australia

Atop our dormant volcano, we are cleansed by the heat
of January—*pasturized*, as a poet put it.

The agisted sheep gnaw the ground, but the grass is eternal.
We name the mountains around us, ignorant of their true names.

The windmills to the southwest—the new horizon—have no names.
We do not want to leave here, which is the point of coming.

(iii) Kawhia, New Zealand

In the afternoon, Carmen sits and drums on a log:
the cows gather to watch her. We are intent on this moment.

What are the stones on your necklace, the figures on your torc?
At the heart of travel is blood and family ties.

How much are we willing to pay for what we want?
In leaving, we leave behind a gift—we hope—not a sorrow.

.

(iv) New York

"Get out of *my* terminal!" shouts the cop in JFK.
It's all street theater here, and underneath, on the E line.

"What's the point of travel?" we ask. Three lines to three points,
only to do it all over again.

The red-tail hawk, with its white speckled breast, takes one stoop
to carry off the sparrow on the railing.

How pointless can it be, when our lives inscribe a triangle,
while we find ourselves at home at the center of ourselves?

Genoa, Italy

IN THE VIA DELLE FONTANE

Each of us must give something, to make sure
that some of us are not forced to give everything.

The graffito is one of many scattered
among lurid murals at street level
on the Via delle Fontane in gritty Genoa.

Advised by police to let the students be,
the University's Faculty of Foreign Languages
yields to Occupied Social Centers in its midst:

Ognuno di noi deve dare qualcosa,
per fare in modo che alcuni di noi
non siano costretti a dare tutto.

"To Carlo" follows—no need for a surname,
everyone here knows who he is,
everyone knows the story. And yet,

who knows but he may have looked back
on that day years later with pride
or perhaps some embarrassment,

hurling an extinguisher at a police van.
Youthful excess, a violent indiscretion, but
in a just cause, even if justice—like Astrea—

left our world a long time ago. He wouldn't
tell his children, of course: parents are meant
to be sober folk, but a friend, or friends,

at table after a bottle of decent local wine.
(You know how conversation can draw you in
and then draw out your foibles and secrets.)

They would have laughed, if ruefully,
for things rarely work out the way we hope,
and the dreams of youth almost never.

And the policeman who shot him point-blank?
What does he tell his friends? He no more
survived than Carlo. His is another story.

GENOA BY THE SEA

"Speak to the Genoese about the sea."
—Leonardo da Vinci

To live between mountain steeps and the deep Ligurian Sea,
where the mountains themselves come sharply down to the sea,
is to face hard choices, is to face, finally, the sea.

So Genoa reversed the inflowing motion of the sea,
going out in waves of war and commerce upon the sea,
financed with a shrewdness born of dealing with the sea.

Thus Genoese headed west to reach India by sea
long before Columbus misconstrued it—all at sea—
caught between his devils and the deep blue sea.

Genoa, a busy port still, sets great store by the sea,
as do tourists, nearby, flocking to bask on rocks by the sea—
though a sea change will come, as temperatures rise with the sea.

O Genoa, Genoa, your painted palaces all face the sea,
as if your future, too, will be discovered by that sea,
borne by emerald cerulean waves of the sea.

THE GENOA GRAIL

"la memoria di tanta grazie"
——Cattedrale di San Lorenzo

I
9 February 1941: Genoa

Light flashing on the surface of the sea,
gentle green swells rising and falling away,
the promise of fair weather, are no guarantee

a sudden turn won't change the day
back to alarms and thumping explosions,
the whistling of shells, the spray

of near misses, the witless emotions.
Force H steams back from Operation Grog
on high alert, going through motions

all but second nature by now in the smog
of war. The carrier and battleships withdraw,
the men at the big guns ready to slog

the intercepting fleet Supermarina—
Italy's Naval High Command—sends out
to avenge the shelling of Genova.

It was a morning's work, brought about
by the need to convince Franco
this was a conflict he'd best sit out.

In three days' time, the Duce, Benito,
will meet the General at Bordighera
to bring Spain in against the Allies. A show

of force, thinks Churchill, on the Riviera
nearby will reveal how unprepared
Mussolini really is. And so Genoa,

with its shipyards and port, has again fared
poorly in this war, bearing the brutal brunt.
The calculation works: Gibraltar is spared.

And at what cost? In opening this front
the British leave unscathed, while the Genoese
suffer a gross of deaths and the affront

of ineffective response. The city seethes
with resentment as Maria José,
Princess of Piedmont, finds it on its knees.

II

17 May 1101: Caesarea

Of Caesarea, much has disappeared:
Roman palaces, the Christian library,
the city walls invaders would have feared,

standing before them at siege, wary
of what stands behind the slotted walls.
Vestiges remain. Time and sand will bury

most things and what—in the present—befalls
us is often what we dig up: the past.
The Pilate Stone, with its inscription, calls

to Christians the way the Minaret once did
to the faithful there in Palestine.
(All these layers of which we are never rid.)

Guglielmo Embriaco, whose design
for the towers that brings Jerusalem down
brings him fame from Tasso, and a name to enshrine

the deed, "mallet head," takes the Muslim town
with Baldwin the First, who, in butchering
the populace, adds to his barbarous renown—

thus shall Crusaders remain the recurring
nightmare of Islam. After fifteen days
the city is ripe for sacking and, during

this plunder, the Genoese, in the craze
for spoils, enrich themselves beyond belief—
or not quite, for it is here that they raise

the ultimate relic, that chalice of grief—
the *Sacro Catino*, or Holy Grail—
the emerald green dish that becomes the chief

ornament of San Lorenzo when they sail
home to Genoa and Embriaco
enters in triumph, glorified by travail.

Napoleon will later take it to show
disdain for the other treasures, only
to break it, dealing the myth a shattering blow.

III
28 October 1998: London

To prolonged applause, Commander Henry Hatfield
stands down as Treasurer of the BAA,
his fellow astronomers, with unconcealed

delight and respect, eager to repay
services rendered with wit and aplomb—
his nine profitable years on display.

An amateur we'd call him, who had become
famous for his *Photographic Lunar Atlas*,
and infamous, too, for a single bomb.

A twenty-year-old midshipman whose progress
must have been rapid, suddenly thrust,
with little training, and under the stress

of combat, into a position of trust:
a Trainer on the *HMS Malaya*,
the naval gunner whose job is to adjust

the calculations of range to pitch and yaw.
At 8:14 firing began in heavy fog,
thirteen miles out from the port of Genoa.

Two salvos for range, then, says the log,
the third slams east of the docks near Polcévera.
(How did they gauge panic in Operation Grog?)

Hatfield corrects to the left for the error,
compounding it, for left is east, not west.
Later salvos blanket the city with terror,

but Hatfield's salvo—to his own confessed
horror—hits the Cathedral San Lorenzo,
busting through the nave—a bullet in the city's chest.

The searing armor-piercing shell, meant to blow
up steel-clad ships, fails to explode on impact—
the ancient masonry too "soft"—and so

the Church survives, with all its loot from the sack
of Holy Lands. "Miraculous," thinks Hatfield,
who becomes a devout Roman Catholic.

Coda
25 September 2013: Genoa

It stands near the main entrance, in the south aisle
(not the sort of icon one would expect)
a shell five feet tall, a lone sentinel

to remind us of miracles and the wreck
of war—as if Genoa needs reminding.
It's not the original shell, some suspect,

since newspapers reported how the thing
was defused, removed and dumped into the sea.
But a British shell it is, and when bells ring

out in the Cathedral tower—key of C
major—does the shell secretly sound,
along with the restored glass Grail, in sympathy?

VFGA

Santa Maria di Castello, Genoa

I cannot paint to save my life, but I will,
ex voto: in fulfillment of the vow.

Who knew you could bargain with a ghost?
I'd give anything, we say, but give up

nothing of any worth. So I gave up
all together, and got nothing in return.

But I made it mine. When I walk in the garden
among tall pines and low flowers,

there is an absence, but I pay it no mind.
That's part of the agreement. Gulls cry out

over the bay, a bird—hidden—chitters to itself,
the early morning mist, pink in the distance, hovers

along the immaculate horizon of the sea,
while traffic and trains race by

in the morning rush to get ahead.
Such things matter little in this afterlife.

To say I gave up on my life wouldn't be true:
it's the other way around. At times,

it feels like freedom, but then it's just a fact
of existing like anything else that dies

or wears down or simply changes
into something else, somewhere else.

My promise was to live if I lived
and not be any of those other people,

the ones I once believed in.
Who cares if I have no skill to render

myself as I am? No one would recognize me
anyway, in my invisibility.

So I have painted this square of wood—
inexpertly, crudely—to tell my story

and acknowledge my good fortune.
Look, in this corner, the vision

of the black Christ—a stand-in for the void
that struck my heart like a viper—

and here, in lurid red, my sickly frame
outstretched upon a simple wooden bed.

The room is otherwise empty, the window blank.
It will do. It's only a reminder, a token

of what really happened, which is simple enough:
I disappeared and went on living—just as I promised.

VFGA: *Votem Fecit Gratium Accepit,*
"Vow made, graces received." There, it's done.

Mont St.-Michel, Normandy

PROLOGUE

Begin with a vision:
In the bay, an island
    embraced by sands, a river
        and the tidal wash of the sea.

Or, begin with fire:
A rock rises, folded forms
    erode and the sea rushes in
        laving the isolate shore.

Begin with a vision:
A sword flames in the dream
    of the bishop—a shooting star
        in a chaos of the sky.

Or begin with what you find:
Shell, sea-bird, shadow,
    rooftop, pillar, steeple,
        someone in a room of stone.

EQUINOX

The tide swells up along the flats at the crescent mouth of the bay,
channels and spillways—cut by freshwater streams and rivers—

inundated by the sea: this is spring tide at Mont St.-Michel,
the waters rising over Easter week flooding the wet sands

around the Mount, as if to cut it off from the mundane world
that flocks to the abbey walls to watch the tide come in, seeing this:

far out in the bay a lip of water glints in the sunlight, moving as a single
wave, flowing like lava down a mountain, but up along the sloping strand

it flows, pushed by the weight of the sea, the sea swollen and stretched
like a membrane about the earth, pulled by the force of the moon,

the moon full in the light of its sun—the sun even now
lending radiance to the surface of sand and water

as the tide's wave advances towards Tombelaine and then
finds the deeper channels of Le Couesnon, La Sélune and La Sée,

picking up speed in the narrow bends of the cuts and breaking into
a turbulence that sends ripples back along the surface like corrugated cardboard

unrolled, and for the first time the sound of the tide is heard, a flash flood
of noise, an agitation in the air that mimics the swirling water as it

froths in the fresher currents and undermines the deep-gouged banks
of sand, its progress an incitement to the blood, as if all

drama adhered to the inevitable: the water flooding everything
in its path, the sea—a river overrunning itself—setting up counter-

currents and eddies, whirlpools and whorls, grinding down the mutable
sands rippled in texture and mirroring the undulations of the roiling water above

in a topography of wind and waves—and then darker the scene as a thick cloud
obscures the sun and colors drain from the crawling surface of the water

shuddering, encroaching on the walls of the Mount itself, slapping
the rocks by the little island-chapel of St. Aubert, and then

as suddenly the light returns, finding a quick opening in the cloud,
picking out, illuminating, the spot on the sands where seagulls gather

noisily, the last spit still showing—but the waves push forward the waves
before and in seconds the gulls lift squawking in protest as their bit disappears

and—but for the digue—the Mount is an island utterly once more and the banks
of the grève delineate the shoreline, as the vascular sea inhabits the bay:

slowly the winds die down while the sun glows yellow-to-orange,
and on the quieting waters a white string of foam—as if cast

on the surface by an angler or angel—drifts with the currents in a lazy line,
and elation, from its flood tide, oscillating in flux and reflux, subsides

to a placid and serene equipoise—a hiatus—before the equinoctial tide
withdraws toward the crescent mouth of the bay, in spring time at Mont St.-Michel.

LOOKING OUT

i

Above the Chatelet, looking out, in early morning,
the sands have a desert aspect, flat, untextured
as yet by the light. But the sands are cold and wet,
with sinuous watercourses glinting like quartz
embedded in the stone walls of the Mount. To the north,
tracks are still visible in the blue-grey mud, marking
the way to Tombelaine and the fringe of the sea.

ii

Off the north face, on a flange of rock—the bridge
of a ship—we stand in exhilarating space,
looking out on mudflats and intricate forms,
of which this shadow we belong to is one, extending
for miles in late afternoon—a benediction,
as if the world, in concert with a shift of perspective,
dilated in a rising breeze, and we sailed with it.

iii

Here looking out for each other is no different
than looking out for ourselves: our purposes conjoined,
our prospects about the same, our differences only
ramifying forms stemming from a single
cause, leading to a singular effect: to be
the object of a scrutiny and the subject of whatever
knowledge these places hold for those who seek them out.

PROCESSION

i

In the slate-gray morning before dawn—
when the paving stones are damp with dew
and the air savors of coffee and bread—
when the day's provisions are stacked against doors
and sparrows peck at the crusts of baguettes—
when a footstep is heard at a distance, echoing,
and every sound's an event—
when shadows cling to the evergreen trees
and the sky glows with an ambient light—
then, in the morning, for moments
at a time, time is momentary.

ii

Everything hinges on the horizon:
at dawn, day opens with a crescent blaze:
granite towers redden, leaded glass coruscates,
rooftops and walkways shine in sudden light.

Moving like clockwork, the circuit of the day
makes a sundial of the Mount, and the spire—
brandishing its gilded archangel—
points to an opposite horizon.

iii

Past the parish church, beyond the last shop,
the Grande-Rue turns steep to the left,
stairs climb to the ramparts and battlements:
with the village behind, the abbey before,
the way leads on counterclockwise—against
the flow of time, concurrent with the past.

iv

The ascent can wind you, take your breath away,
as vistas come into sight—and, into focus:
the intricate complex of the abbey.

To marvel here is to join the perennial pilgrimage,
retracing the steps of other unremarkable ones
who long since vanished in their turn.

Catch your breath, and try to take in—as though
aspiring to nothing less—the whole of what you find
above, below and at your fingertips.

You are but midway.

Shiprock, New Mexico

NOON

Earth, air and water
and out of the element fire

comes light. Light floods
the desert the way a tide

inundates salt flats—
filling the expanse with

a mutable surface.
High up, looking out:

the valleys around—from
Rattlesnake to Redrock—

shimmer. Earth, air and water,
and from out the element fire

comes the noonday heat
in waves.

HALF-LIGHT

Here we find the future—
  it is much like the past:
plateaus abraded by the wind,
  hills blanched by sunlight,
bones on the desert floor.

Climbing to the base
  of the vertical wall:
a room like a cave appears,
  flanked by grasping shrubs
and a large rounded stone.

Crouching, I inspect
  a handful of debris:
coarse and fine-grained sands,
  pale brown to deep red,
with shiny flecks intermixed.

Once I thought darkness
  the opposite of light.
The rock disabused me.
  Night enfolds day,
as day unfolds into night.

REVELATION FROM BELOW

The desert converges from a distance upon the rock,
as when a cathedral organizes a plain or plateau,
or an oak tree a field: drawing down the sky,
delimiting a new horizon.

The rock is revealed as the land wears away,
its shape weathered by wind and rain,
the sandstone eroding endlessly around it.
Were the desert illusory, the rock would be real.

We too are of the ground. A stone, a twig, a tiny bloom
will hold us among vast surfaces undulating
in morning light. Though we cannot see it from here,
out upon the desert floor the rock casts its shadow.

RECOGNITION

What flows between us under the ground of feeling?
The elements are all in motion: the air as wind,
rainwater trickling, folds of igneous rock—fire once
as molten earth—radiant now in fading light.

Under the ground of feeling, what flows between us
is a sound beneath silence, felt not heard, a presence—
like the rock—vibrating at a frequency so fine
we cannot miss it and cannot apprehend it.

Below feeling, what flows between us is the ground
of our living, with elemental motions binding
us together, turning with the earth as far as time
and as long as space fold us within as one.

What flows between us under the ground of feeling?
From a distance, westward looking back, the rock cascades
in forms, not static or finished, but waiting on change.
No finer thought, no truer feeling, than recognition.

THE DIKES

Like a stone jetty, curving out into a sandy bay,
or the arm of a spiral nebula light-years away,

the volcanic dikes branch off at oblique
angles from the rock, as though to seek

out new ground or build up fortress walls.
Up close they look man-made, cathedrals

in ruins or an ancient archeological site.
But from a distance, wings; or from a height,

the tail of a primitive beast.
But now, as shadows grow from the east,

the dikes are the stopped hands of a clock,
sundials with noon zero at the rock.

Later, as evening drops suddenly to night,
winds along the walls lift into flight.

THE IMAGINED WORLD

At night the sky lights up
              an imagined world reflecting
this unimaginable one.

No mysteries here,
              only the puzzle of the sky
and the rock in silhouette.

As the moon rises
              shadows deepen,
and creatures hold their breath.

Step out into the light, be known.

When the wind swirls
              in a pillar of dust,
look up: the sky is strewn with stars.

There is a pattern to life
              discernible at a distance
but only grasped in a glimpse.

If I turn my back
              and look at the risen moon,
the rock abides.

THE WIND AT YOUR BACK

A beginning but not a beginning—
when beginnings are ends.
                                    And so you climb,
with care, the eastern flank—detritus
the rock has cast from itself—until at last,
what do you find?
                                    A height that bewilders
the sense of scale, a distance out of all
proportion, and swallows diving, sweeping
about, curious as to intrusions
or simply marking another presence
along the cliff face.
                                    You are no farther
than the base of the rock, where it rises
out of its skirt of debris vertical,
vertiginous, a wall to your effort.
Here, where it begins, you can go no further—
yet sensing to what end you undertook
the climb, you delight in the swallows,
the soaring sky, and the wind at your back.

Mt. Glasgow, Australia

A CONSTANT REFRAIN

The winds are constant up this high:
they shift from north to south and west.
North brings heat and south the rain,
but day to day—as year to year—
who knows which way they'll blow?

The drought is constant out this way:
in summer the pastures black or brown—
brown for cattle and black for sheep, as
farmers graze by agistment. Clouds appear—
who knows if rain will follow?

The land is constantly changing here:
all day long the sky lights up a different
view of what it means to live in a land
that's changed by use. What use is it to know?
Change has changed the wind and rain.

AN INVITATION

In winter on Mt. Glasgow
there are mornings, before
the sun has risen high,
when mist like smoke
in the small declivities
between the hills spreads
out as a haze of fog, softening
the aspect of the view.
For those living in Clunes
and Talbot, in low-lying lands,
the day is damp and cloudy.
That will change by noon,
as the sun lifts the fog,
brightening the day towards
sunshine and the sharp clarity
of a high blue sky.
But up here, the future presides
already, for we can see
what others can't, that it's
just a matter of time.
You can wait it out below, or
you can come here and sit
with us on the deck, having
coffee and some lemon cake,
perfecting the day.

IN EXTREMIS

The brown snake swished away from under
the steps, startled by my tromping down.
To be fearless here is foolish,
so I watch my step in the stony paddock.

That same day, when I drove up the drive,
there was a conference of magpies
by the deck—dozens in fact—no doubt
discussing the brown snake's arrival.

If only I could have listened in, I'd have
been the wiser for it. But they flew or hopped
away and I was left to my own surmises.
Now, hawks ply the insinuating updrafts:

I wouldn't want to be a rodent on this
mountain, or anything low on the food chain.
We live among elements, any one of which
could take us in a moment.

WINTER FOG

It's as if the clouds hadn't descended
but rose up from out of the land,
a thick substance drawn from the marrow
of this rock ribbed mountain.

The land makes clouds,
as if to begin all over again
the drift of things, without
any sign of humanity.

It's not that we haven't woken up:
we haven't begun to exist, so primeval
is the sight, with no lights visible
from distant settlements in the valley.

And now, even we begin to be
enfolded, as the fog bank rises,
an incipient dawn. It is like sleep
or a slow swoon, a haze upon the sight.

Nothing is seen beyond
the precipitant edge of our land,
the ghostly trees and stone wall
turning into eerie emblems.

Deep in the cloudbank, we could be
anywhere or nowhere.
There is a bright glow to the east,
but there will be no dawn today.

PAST COOBER PEDY

Along the highway cars are fewer than roadkill.
Eagles attend to corpses and crows crowd around.

Wedge-tails play chicken with us as they lift away
just in time. Out here, though, nothing is just in time.

Occasionally, we pass a cow upended in a paddock.
At dusk, we stop to let the road trains do their work.

IRONBARK POPPY

for Les Murray

All day long he laid into it like one
possessed or trying to possess what he
couldn't own. That he couldn't own up to
a lack accounted for the fury of the blows.
It was spring, and the reddish-pink "rosea"
flowers buzzed with bees high above, and once,
at noon, a regent honeyeater made a rare
appearance, while parrots chortled "mugga"
and bellbirds beyond kept a random tally.
Thwack! went the axe, but the black bark took
the blade and gave it back a little duller.
Thwack! A few cuts sliced into wood
and sap wept mournful slow, but
deeper in was tougher stuff and drew
first blood from his blistered hands.
Anger burned him from within as the sun
stung his skin and the sweat in his eyes
was like salt in a wound. It was personal.
He'd say otherwise, that for the good
of the stand this one had to go, towering
above the others, stunting their growth.
But nature enforces a harsh equilibrium
and what grows high into the light is
a magnificence in a working forest.
Birds sing beyond their need, for pleasure,
and the great tree exfoliates with joy,
as in the parable of the talents.
The Ironbark, at one ton per square meter,
was too much for the diminished man, who
buried the head of his axe in the ground
and walked out of the woods, exhausted,
in the end, by the ignorance of his folly.

III

Nothing Gold Can Stay

HARD LIGHT IN THE GOLDFIELDS

In the far, far distance, just below
the lowering sky, with its wash of blue
and gray, a line of light appears, as if
pressed down upon the land and spreading
horizontally along the long horizon.
And in that narrow band, white clouds shine,
the inverse of the dark hills surrounding them.
What isn't a sign these days? Has hope
diminished to that extent, that a mere
streak of light is set upon as evidence
that all is not darkness? That the times
may yet turn around and dawn burn brighter?
And if the world in its indifference
can bring us comfort, what need have we
of benevolence? The sky-gods withdrew
a long time ago, but that streak of light—
how it answers to a need, and the need
answerable to neither hope nor faith,
but to the ground of being in the world.
That we should exist at all seems unaccountable:
a happy accident, we say—though no one believes
it at heart. Were it not for all our cruelty,
we might live in grace, as hatred is darkness,
and darkness the absence of light.
We cannot get behind this world, only
deeper into it, until—inside out—its strangeness
is revealed and every prospect, every certainty
we thought we knew, turns foreign to us,
and fresh, like that band of light and those
rising clouds. It is only when hope falls away
that there is any hope. Look hard at the world—
says the world—it is yourself.

A TRACE OF DOUBT

Earliest morning, before pre-dawn pale light,
darkness lit up by stars and the diffuse

glow of towns miles away—like false
dawns, the light fading instead of spreading,

as when hope turns out to be fear
and sinks into its own night or season

of dismay. Stars, then, and a wisp of star
cloud still visible, a galaxy of galaxies.

The planets are the brightest, and the nearest,
like sentinels, all attention.

The stars, skittish, turn away when
you look at them directly. Better to

notice sidelong when they come into
themselves, as do some people when they

think no one is watching them. The light
of the eye puts out the stars, when seeing

is truant to looking, the eye no longer
a receptacle. Just now, a streaking,

a white-hot wire half glimpsed, then gone—
a shooting star, a fallen angel, a flash

in the eye—who's to know? It happens or it
doesn't, and only assent makes it real,

a trace of light streaming across the mind.

ON A MOUNTAINTOP AT NIGHT

i.m. Joseph Brodsky

Is that despair? you asked.
Is that disaster?
The stars of this southern sky
might answer your question. But how
many of them—light years away—
are extinguished? Every year light
on a darkening road, and every
poet—let's say true poet—
Diogenes with his lamp.
                    We look to stars,
not for comfort, of course, or knowledge,
but for a sense that we are of this moment
and no part of futurity, just one of
a drift of infinitesimal particles—
unless, that is, we have done other
than the possible, about which
poets affect silence, while all along
mouthing those dark syllables heard
as night falls, the god-like voices
murmuring a secret name, a final hope.

AT A CROSSROADS NEAR DELPHI

> For in real tragedy, it is not the hero who perishes:
> it is the Chorus.
> —Joseph Brodsky

We live without heroes now—just as well,
you say—yet in that absence it is we
who perish. Not all at once, of course,
but singly, or in pairs, unnoted by the many,
with only a few friends and family to mourn us.
It is in the nature of things that this obtains,
neither judgment nor law but out of the indifference
of gods who have their own scenes to play out.
> *O roads that lead away,*
> *Which way are we to turn?*

All this we foresaw, and raised our voices
in despair, some ready to throw themselves
upon the advancing machinery—it runs
on blood and leaves a slick behind.
To act has done our hearts good, but it
drives us mad to think what might have been
or what will be. Exposed in our roles,
we fear most the forgetfulness of others—
that it will all have been in vain, knowing
it was all in vain to begin with.
> *O roads that lead away,*
> *Which way are we to turn?*

Time was, our numbers gave us strength, but now,
dwindled, a mere glint in the eye will start the dogs.
You say we were always ineffectual, but we knew
the truth in the end, as bodies were carted off.
We're moving to a different stage now where speech,
like a form of silence or an exhalation, is emptied out

and carries with the wind along these dusty roads.
But look!—down the way—torches advancing.

> O road that leads our way,
> Which way are we to turn?

FROM *EUGENE ONEGIN*
V:1

In that year, the autumn weather
held on a long time,
waiting and waiting for winter.
Snow first fell in January
on the third, at night. And, waking early,
Tatyana through the window sees
the morning white in the courtyard:
flowerbeds, roofs and the fence,
thin designs on the window glass,
trees in winter-silence,
the magpies merry in the courtyard,
and softly strewn, the mountains
shining in carpets of snow.
Everywhere radiance: all is white.

THE END OF WINTER

This is the end of winter.
Snow dissolves into ground water
and the swollen streams make rapids
where weeks before there was ice.

Does with fawns become bolder,
woodchucks emerge and the slow possum.
As for birds, new sounds declare
the season's turn: they carry spring

on their wings and call for the green blush.
But it is not spring. Nor is it the end of winter,
but winter's end, loosening its clutch of cold.
Change takes time, and time, what is it

but change? The clock means nothing.
Only at a great distance does it all stand still.

THE WOLF TREE

The wolf tree was an oak, allowed to grow
along a pasture line marked by a stone fence

deep now in the woods, the woods deep in snow.
It is the first of March, and in the present tense

of memory, it will always be that year
when everything changed, and change made sense.

In the open field, the oak was in the clear
to spread its lateral branches like outstretched arms.

A lone giant back then, a sheer
delight to behold, an icon for the farms

around: free, proud and unencumbered.
But now, a century later, its bucolic charms

are hidden by what has occurred,
hedged round by a forest of younger trees

competing for the light, since no herd
browsed them down, so no cold could freeze

them out nor wind-whipped grass fire
cleanse the undergrowth of saplings, twigs and leaves.

All the green growth is in the higher
branches now, as the wolf tree was forced

to grow vertical again, and in that dire
condition, withdraw the life-source

from the horizontal limbs
shaded in the darkened forest.

Along the branches, where the light swims
in dappled shade, you can see where the tree,

in closing down, trims
itself—like amputations at the knees

in field hospitals in a war zone.
Vestigial now, each branch—an amputee's

useless limb—is left alone
to its fated fall, while the tree, living on

in this second growth forest, is unknown
except for the chance traveler who—coming upon

it in the midst of the thick woods—stands
and wonders how came this virtual mastodon

of an oak to live here, so deep in the uplands.

A LIGHT BREEZE IS BEST

Pleasant is preferable to pleasure,
as joy is to enjoyment.
A still summer morning
before the imposition of wind.
Clouds stretched thin, as if
distorted in a mirror
or like the ground
of feeling before thought.
My mind is a wind.
It forecasts change,
a harbinger of itself.
A light breeze is best,
intermittent, sociable
like conversation that
falls still and rises upon
impulse—from where
I do not know but only
obey as a law of myself.
Golden grass among newer green
waves back and forth
but tends to one direction,
the prevailing weather,
the fine seed heads bent
toward the ground, like
yearning or old remembrance.
This is a cure of the land,
adequate in spite of
commotions I have known.
A light breeze is best.

AUBADE: SUN SONG

What we grow out of—if we move on—
is what we grew out of in the first place.

To leave ourselves behind: the double gesture,
to replicate and to shed the husk of certainty.

Another morning risen upon the world:
the sun, unobstructed, becomes the singular

presence in this simple room of windows and white walls.
Overnight, heavy dew left lights winking in the grass

where the wind now threshes with a swirling motion.
You cannot hide from the sun, not for long.

Like air, like water, light finds its way in,
the antiseptic to the wounds we dress daily.

Our virtues mask the deepest cuts.
O welcome, sun, blaze me to the bone.

SUNSCAPE

Already the sky is blue green
as the disc of the sun

appears, a glowing dot,
a miniature of itself.

Within seconds, you cannot
look at it directly or everything

glows an afterimage.
What we see by, we turn

away from, knowing it by glimpses,
or not knowing it at all.

The world is so visibly
so much the case that it seems

as if the sun were looking at us.
And now, roused by the light,

the wind rises in response,
as day defines itself.

How incommensurable this day,
this privilege of living one more,

before that day when we return
to the stellar dust we came from.

NOTHING GOLD CAN STAY

On the high field overlooking our hollow,
with new grass already thick and the April
sun unfamiliarly warm, we three hiked
about in conversation until I stopped
and recited that New England poem of Frost's
with its declension of grief in the midst
of golden hopes, but, as I spoke the last
line, you turned away sharply, as if
stung by a pain too private to share or
even acknowledge. It seemed a mistake, then,
to have said that poem with your happiness so
unmitigated, as if rolling the apple
of discord into the celebration in
that ancient myth, though I meant no harm.
Later, when I learned you left your partner
of so many years suddenly, and then,
when I met him—not as before content,
but inconsolable and bewildered by loss—
I recalled that day in a different light,
as the dawn of a decision you had made
already, that neither love nor anything
gold could make you stay.

TRAVELS WITH F. E.

All our trips tended south toward the sea
and overseas: first Mexico, in the Yucatan,
then Hawaii, on Kauai's north shore, and next
Fiji, to a little island off a larger one, and finally
Australia, down the bay from Melbourne.
We visited once in Cape Cod, but that was
domestic, not international, a family affair.
Warm water was the point, with a beach, some books
and conviviality that rose with Manhattans at five.
Planning the trip was as good as going—anticipating
pleasure a pleasure in itself, and a good deal easier.
If traveling's a fool's paradise, what is hell?
As there's no special circle for the travel agent,
they ought to all be consigned to Limbo
with hapless victims at a luggage carousel.
But mishaps were always taken in stride
because your step never faltered—not until the end,
when you couldn't stand, and couldn't stand that,
so died instead the very next day, as much
to control your death as you did your life.
To live was to swim against the tide, and swimming
was your particular joy, best when buoyed
by salt water, which you breasted like a swan.
Floating must have been liberating for someone
so down to earth the local minister was relieved
when you relieved him of his pastoral duties—
your faith, you said, was larger than his church—
and really it was about the music in the end,
the only proof of God you ever needed
as a member of the choir. We only ever added
our voice to yours, and on those travels
we were the chorus, too, and you our song.

ON THE RADIO

All summer long those afternoons
the transistor radio crackling

with voices from Boston, Detroit,
Washington and New York—

Brooklyn and The Bronx.
"How about that!" came the call.

My grandfather hated Mel Allen—
I never knew why—

since why was a question I never asked.
The world was the way it was

and I simply thrown into it
with no say, no knowledge or understanding—

save the ability to turn a double play
or lay down a drag bunt for a hit.

My grandfather could throw a knuckleball.
Catch made him happy, as if tossing

away care and getting solace back each time.
At my age now, he was dying—

though we didn't know it—
a disease of the blood aged him.

So he sat, or drove, with that radio—
a Zenith was it, or a Philips?—

its worn leather case protecting it,
lending a dignity he always conveyed.

Catching sight of it afterwards was like seeing
a potent memory sitting on a shelf.

CO. KERRY

i.m. Peter Steele

The very smell of the sea beckons—
pungent, redolent of other shores.

I walk the beach with my forebears.
They set off and I returned.

We have found one another out.

The lighthouse at Fenit
looks in all directions at once:

comings and goings its only concern.
This is a place of stone.

This is where the long view obtains.

Limestone conglomerate
holds it all together.

Beyond the farthest reach of this ocean,
someone dear is fading fast away.

He may even be gone as I say these words.

His faith is that he has always been the life
that is leaving him, leaving us.

The sea beckons. The lighthouse is dark.
Clouds obscure the high hills, the wind is steady.

This is where we find ourselves.

IV

Hafiz: Ghazals

HAFIZ: GHAZAL 1

O Saqi, hand round to me that cup of wine,
    for love seemed easy at first, but then grew hard.

How full of anguish are those who wait for the eastern breeze
    to bring a scent of musk from the twist of her dark hair.

If the Master tells you, stain your prayer mat with wine,
    for such a traveler is not ignorant of the road or of its stations.

At her caravanserai, what chance have we to woo her,
    when every moment the bells ring out, "pack up the camels"?

The dark night, the fearful waves, the terror of the whirlpool,
    how can they, who go lightly along the shore, know our condition?

Through self-indulgence, my name is held in disrepute.
    How long can our assemblies keep hidden our joyous secret?

Hafiz, if you so desire her presence, do not hide from Him:
    when you find your beloved, abandon the world—let it go.

HAFIZ: GHAZAL 11

Saqi, kindle our cup with the blazing light of wine.
    Minstrel, sing of how the world has gone our way.

You, unaware of our joy in perpetual drinking,
    we have seen the beloved reflected in our cup.

The coy glances and charms of the willowy ones cease
    when our graceful cypress sways into view.

He whose heart is enlivened with love will never die.
    Our immortality is registered in the ledger of the world.

On the day of judgment, I fear the sheik's lawful bread
    will have no more value than our forbidden wine.

In the eyes of our beloved, our drunkenness is pleasing.
    That is why we have given full rein to intoxication.

O breeze, if you pass over the rose beds of the beloved,
    take care to convey our message.

Say, "Why do you deliberately forget our name?
    The time will come of itself when no one remembers."

Hafiz, go on, scatter the grain of your tears.
    Perhaps the bird of union will fly to our snare.

HAFIZ: GHAZAL 34

For the recluse, what need is there for diversions?
    Who needs wilderness when the street of the beloved is at hand?

O beloved, by the need you have for God,
    ask, for a moment at least, what we need.

O king of beauty, by God have we burned!
    Ask, please, "What does the beggar need?"

Need is our inheritance, but we have no language for begging.
    In the presence of the Merciful One, what need is there for pleading?

If you intend to take our life, there's no need for pretense:
    when the goods belong to you, what need is there for plunder?

The world-revealing magic cup is the luminous heart of my beloved.
    What point is there, then, in revealing my need?

I am no longer under obligation to the fisherman:
    once the pearl is harvested, who needs the sea?

O beggar-lover, when the soul-giving lip of the beloved
    knows your need, what point is there in asking?

Go, impostor, I have nothing to do with you.
    Friends are here. I have no need for enemies.

Hafiz, end this now. Genius will become clear by itself.
    Who needs to quarrel and contend with an impostor?

HAFIZ: GHAZAL 37

Come, for the palace of hope has weak foundations.
    Bring wine, for life's foundations are built on wind.

I am the slave of he who, under the azure wheel of the sky,
    is free of what takes the tint of attachment.

How shall I tell you the good news I received from that unseen angel
    in the tavern last night, when I was drunk and ruined?

"O royal falcon of lofty vision," it said, "worthy of the sacred tree of Sidra,
    this corner of woe is not your nest.

"On the battlements of Heaven they are whistling to recall you.
    What can it be that ensnares you here?"

I will give you some advice; remember and apply it,
    for it comes from the Master of my way:

"Do not expect constancy in an unstable world,
    this hag is the bride of a thousand lovers."

Grieve not for the grief of the world, nor forget my counsel,
    for I recall this loving subtlety from a traveler on the way:

"Be content with what is given you, loosen the knot of your brow.
    The gate of choice is not open to you and me."

In the smile of the rose, there is no trace of loyalty or fidelity:
    cry, O nightingale, for this is the place for lamenting.

O, weak poet, why do you envy Hafiz?
    The acceptance of the heart and the grace of speech are God-given.

HAFIZ: GHAZAL 73

The way of love has no shore.
  There is no help but to surrender your soul.

Every moment you give up your heart to love is joyful.
  To do what is auspicious requires no divination.

Follow the *rend*'s way. It is a track,
  like a trail to buried treasure, not obvious to all.

Do not frighten us with reason's prohibitions, bring wine.
  That bailiff has no jurisdiction in our province.

One can discern Him, like the new moon, with a clear eye.
  The splendor of that sliver of moon does not dwell in every eye.

Ask of your own, "Who is slaying us?"
  O soul, it is not the sin of fortune nor the fault of stars.

The weeping of Hafiz has no effect on you at all.
  I am amazed at that heart, as hard as stone.

HAFIZ: GHAZAL 75

The products from the workshop of the universe, all of it is nothing.
    Bring wine, for the goods of the world are nothing.

The heart and soul long for the honor of intimacy with the beloved.
    That is all, for otherwise heart and soul would be nothing.

Do not, for the sake of shade, be indebted to the sacred trees of Sidra and Túbá:
    when you look closely, O flowing cypress, heavenly trees are nothing.

Five days you are spared in this way station.
    Rest easy awhile, for time is nothing.

O Saqi, we are waiting on the shore by the sea of annihilation.
    Regard it, for the space between lip and mouth is nothing.

Wailing and weeping have sadly consumed me,
    but to narrate or explain is worth nothing.

Fakir, beware: do not grow complacent in your zeal.
    The distance from your cloister to the Magi's tavern is nothing.

The name of Hafiz has gained honor in the world,
    but among *rends*, the calculations of profit and loss are nothing.

HAFIZ: GHAZAL 91

O hoopoe of the east wind, I send you to the Queen of Sheba.
　　Behold from whence, and to where, I send you.

It is a pity a bird like you should reside on this trash heap of grief.
　　From here I am sending you to a nest of constancy.

On love's path, there is no stage of either near or far.
　　I see you clearly, and I send a prayer to you.

Every morning and evening I send you a caravan of prayers
　　in the company of the north and east winds.

So long as the army of grief spares the kingdom of my heart,
　　I will provision you with the precious store of my life.

Saqi, come! for the voice of the hidden one brought me good news:
　　"Be patient in pain, for I am issuing you a remedy."

O hidden one, now my heart's companion,
　　I pray for you and send you greetings.

See, in your own face, the creating force of God,
　　for I am sending you a God-revealing mirror.

And that the minstrels may tell you of my passion for you,
　　I send ghazals and qawls for instruments and voices.

Hafiz, the song of our assembly is the recitation of your goodness.
　　Hurry, I am sending you a horse and a robe.

HAFIZ: GHAZAL 102

May your body not need the physician's care,
    your delicate life safe from injury.

The health of all horizons depends upon your health.
    May your person be untroubled by any illness.

When autumn comes to plunder this meadow,
    may it not find its way to the straight and lofty cypress.

In that place where your beauty displays its splendor,
    may the pessimist and ill-wisher have no power of reproach.

The perfection of form and substance is secured by your well-being.
    May your outer appearance and inward state be free of damage and dejection.

Whoever looks with vicious eyes upon your moon-like face,
    may his life be nothing but wild rue burnt in your ritual fire.

Seek healing from the sugar-scattered words of Hafiz.
    May you never be in need of the rose-water and candy cure.

HAFIZ: GHAZAL 151

If I go after her, she stirs up a fuss.
   And if I hang back, she rises in wrath.

And if, in desire, for a moment on the road,
   I fall as dust at her feet, she flees like the wind.

And if I seek but half a kiss, a hundred evasions
   pour out like sugar from the pearl case of her mouth.

That deceit I see in your eyes
   will muddy many a reputation in the dust of the road.

The steeps and descents of love's desert are calamitous snares.
   Where is the lionhearted one fearless of such affliction?

Ask for a long life and much patience, for Heaven is a trickster
   who will conjure a thousand games stranger than these.

Hafiz, lay your head down on the threshold of submission,
   for if you fight, fate will fight back.

HAFIZ: GHAZAL 179

Last night I saw angels knock at the tavern door:
    Adam's clay had been kneaded and molded into a cup.

Those veiled dwellers of the chaste and sacred sanctuary of Heaven
    drank the intoxicating wine with me, a beggar of the road.

Heaven couldn't bear the burden of His trust,
    so they cast lots and drew the name of me, the mad one.

Forgive the infighting of the seventy-two sects:
    they did not see the truth, so took errant ways.

Thank God, peace has fallen between Him and me.
    The Houris, dancing, have drained the cup in gratitude.

How can we help but be distracted by a thousand thoughts
    when all it took to waylay Adam was a single grain of wheat?

Fire is not the flame with which the candle laughs.
    Fire is what annihilates the moth.

No one has unveiled the face of thought like Hafiz
    since the tresses of speech were first combed with a pen.

HAFIZ: GHAZAL 262

From the rose garden of the world, one rosy cheek is enough for us.
In this meadow, the shade of the flowing cypress is enough.

May I never mingle with the company of hypocrites.
Of all the heavy things in the world, a full cup is enough for me.

The palace of paradise is the reward for good works.
For us *rends* and beggars, the Magian's tavern house is enough.

Sit by the edge of the stream and watch life pass by.
This sign of the fleeting world is enough for us.

Look at the cash in the world's bazaar, and the pain in the world.
If all this profit and loss is not enough for you, it is enough for us.

The beloved is with us. What more do we need?
The fortune of friendship with our soul's companion is enough.

Here I am at your door. For God's sake, don't send me to Heaven.
As for being and abiding, the end of your street is enough for us.

Hafiz, it is unjust to complain of the wellsprings of your fate.
Flowing ghazals and a character pure as water are enough for us.

HAFIZ: GHAZAL 373

I have said it many times and I'll say it again:
  I, the lost one, do not walk this path of my own free will.

They have kept me like a parrot on the other side of the mirror.
  What the Master of eternity tells me to say, I say.

Whether I am the thorn or the rose, there is a Gardener
  by whose hand I was nurtured and grew.

O friends, do not criticize me, bereft in heart and crazed.
  I have a jewel and seek a man of discernment.

Although the wine's color doesn't go with a holy man's cloak,
  do not find fault with me. I use it to wash away the color of hypocrisy.

The laughter and tears of lovers belongs elsewhere.
  I sing in the night, and moan at daybreak.

Hafiz said to me, "Do not sniff at the dust of the tavern door."
  But I say, "Do not blame me, for I smell the fabled musk of Khotan."

AFTER HAFIZ: A WINTER'S DAY

If I could dream of you I would,
    to call up your face in its expressiveness

as poets are wont to do in words: full red lips, bright
    laughing smile, limpid blue eyes, etc.—

and I would be happy in my fascination,
    my wish simply to look at you and see

how your life moves through you,
    a breeze across a flower garden midsummer.

Such a simple joy, really, simple enough
    to water eyes and start a longing

in the heart—a yearning for whatever beauty
    surpasses desire, some excess of love

that cannot be expressed and merely is.
    O, what a dream of dreams that would be!

But sleep is another realm, subject to laws
    I cannot bend or change, as I am subject too,

my will of no account, my wants beyond
    my grasp, and you beyond my reach.

In the gray light of the new day, Hafiz is made ridiculous:
    empty, forlorn, his eyes fixed on the horizon.

V

Seven Catastrophes in Four Movements

SEVEN CATASTROPHES IN FOUR MOVEMENTS

"The most beautiful aesthetic theory in the world."
—Salvador Dali

I   Fold
At the instant,
    the flash of wing, a glint of glass,
the negative is the stable value—
    not this, not that,
          the cleansing of the lens.

    A mere channel is not the sea,
    you apart are not a part of me.

At zero, we break out:
    zero times zero.

Time zero.

At the vanishing point,
    we fold into the Blue Sky.

II   Cusp

(i)
You cannot see it coming,
    pitchfork lightning
        stabs at the ground,
    high intensity smoldering lines
        scorch the ground.

The point is the point
        of no return.

(ii)

Push it beyond:
    a whimpering dog turns and snarls,
    the cowering mob rises and tears
        the rider from his horse.

If you cannot see it for what it is,
you cannot see it coming.

You stand one step
        from the edge.

III   *Swallowtail*

(i)

All the important changes
    are small:
        a flick of the tail at 30k,
        flight another dimension.

The chaos of the night sky,
    a luminous law.

(ii)

Dali's last painting:
    dying solves the riddling equation.

Split the difference,
    you will never be the same,
        alight
           on the swallow's wing.

IV   *Butterfly*

(i)

In the eye of the storm
    you see
           everything
reflected back.

A lucid dream, an awakening,
    you are seen
           for what you are.

(ii)

Time is motion,
           time is thought.
All around you,
           devastated.

Stand still, like a tree,
           and sway,
    give way
    to whatever is given.

Zhuangzi dreamt the "great dream."

In the wild of the blue sky
           the horizon line
                    vanishes

A DAY IN MARCH

for Tina

When were we fully alive?
Did we know it at the time
for what it was? Moments
worth the living. And now,
at the end of time, what
can be cherished for itself
that isn't a forestalling?

O memory, leave me, leave me.

The winter sun is warm
on my face.
                    No, don't leave.

Notes

"In the Via delle Fontane"
Carlo Guiliani, a student protesting a meeting of the Group of Eight in Genoa in 2001, was shot and killed by a police officer.

"Mont St.-Michel, Normandy"
Legend has it that, in AD 708, St. Aubert had three dreams in which he was visited by the Archangel Michael and directed to establish an abbey on Mont St.-Michel, a small island off the coast of Normandy.

"Shiprock, New Mexico"
Shiprock is a Navajo sacred site in the New Mexico desert. A volcanic formation, over 1,700 feet high, it has radiating dikes that extend far out into the desert.

"An Invitation"
Mt. Glasgow is located in the goldfields area of Central Victoria, north of Melbourne, Australia. My wife and I built a house there.

"The Wolf Tree"
A Wolf Tree is an unusually large tree that dominates an area of woods.

"On the Radio"
Mel Allen was a long-time radio and television announcer for the New York Yankees.

"Hafiz: Ghazals"
Hafiz of Shiraz, whose full name was Khwájeh Shamsu'd-Din Muhammad, lived in Iran from about 1325 until 1389. Although the term "hafiz" denotes someone who knows the Koran by heart, the poet took it for his pen name and has been known by it ever since.

Saqi: cup bearer; a boy who pours wine in a tavern; here used as a proper name as well.

rend: hedonistic derelict; a vagabond; a man of no account.

Sidra and Túbá: the tree of Sidra is where Archangel Gabriel appeared before Muhammad; the Túbá tree grows in Heaven.

qawl: short lyric poem

Houris: beautiful young women who are the "pure companions" of the faithful in paradise.

Khotan: the finest musk was said to come from Khotan in Xinjiang, China.

"Seven Catastrophes in Four Movements"
Catastrophe Theory is a mathematical formalization of the seven bifurcation patterns by which systems reach dynamic "tipping points" and transform themselves suddenly into antithetically different states. It was developed by René Thom and Christopher Zeeman in the 1960s and 1970s. Catastrophe Theory has been applied to diverse phenomena, including optics and oscillations, territoriality in animals, crowd behavior, the collapse of regimes and empires, psychological stress, as well as "peak experiences." The four main types of catastrophes are referred to by descriptors suggestive of their geometric representations: fold, cusp, swallowtail, and butterfly.

About the Author

VINCENT MANZI

PAUL KANE has published five collections of poems and ten other books. He has received a Fulbright award, Guggenheim and NEH Fellowships, grants from the Mellon Foundation, a residency from the Bogliasco Foundation, and an honorary doctorate from La Trobe University. Kane is poetry editor for *Antipodes,* artistic director for the Mildura Writers Festival, and general editor of The Braziller Series of Australian Poets. He is currently a professor of English and Environmental Studies at Vassar College and divides his time between homes in Warwick, NY, and Central Victoria in Australia.